Ruth

DISCOVER TOGETHER BIBLE STUDY SERIES

Leader's guides are available at www.discovertogetherseries.com

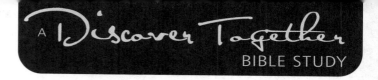

A Discover Together
BIBLE STUDY

Ruth

Discovering God's Faithfulness in an Anxious World

Sue Edwards

KREGEL
PUBLICATIONS

Ruth: Discovering God's Faithfulness in an Anxious World
© 2020 by Sue Edwards

Published by Kregel Publications, a division of Kregel Inc., 2450 Oak Industrial Dr. NE, Grand Rapids, MI 49505.

The author and publisher are not engaged in rendering medical or psychological services, and this book is not intended as a guide to diagnose or treat medical or psychological problems. If medical, psychological, or other expert assistance is required, the reader should seek the services of a health-care provider or certified counselor.

The Cataloging-in-Publication Data is on file with the Library of Congress.

ISBN 978-0-8254-2553-0

Printed in the United States of America
20 21 22 23 24 25 26 27 28 29 / 5 4 3 2 1

Contents

How to Get the Most Out of a Discover Together Bible Study

Women today need Bible study to keep balanced, focused, and Christ-centered in their busy worlds. The tiered questions in *Ruth: Discovering God's Faithfulness in an Anxious World* allow you to choose a depth of study that fits your lifestyle, which may even vary from week to week, depending on your schedule.

Just completing the basic questions will require about an hour per lesson and will provide a basic overview of the text. For busy women, this level offers in-depth Bible study with a minimum time commitment.

"Digging Deeper" questions are for those who want to, and make time to, probe the text even more deeply. Answering these questions may require outside resources such as an atlas, Bible dictionary, or concordance; you may be asked to look up parallel passages for additional insight; or you may be encouraged to investigate the passage using an interlinear Greek-English text or *Vine's Expository Dictionary*. This deeper study will challenge you to learn more about the history, culture, and geography related to the Bible, and to grapple with complex theological issues and differing views. Some with teaching gifts and an interest in advanced academics will enjoy exploring the depths of a passage and might even find themselves creating outlines and charts and writing essays worthy of seminarians!

This inductive Bible study is designed for both individual and group discovery. There are six lessons on the book of Ruth, with two additional, optional lessons you can choose to study. While Lessons 7 and 8 also focus on the topic of anxiety, they offer teachings from other books of the Bible that provide clear, directive, motivational instruction on finding freedom from anxiety. You will benefit most if you tackle each week's lesson on your own and then meet with other women to share insights, struggles, and aha moments. Bible study leaders will find a free, downloadable leader's guide for each study, along with general tips for leading small groups, at www.discovertogetherseries.com.

Choose a realistic level of Bible study that fits your schedule. You may want to finish the basic questions first and then "dig deeper" as time permits. Take time to savor the questions, and don't rush through the

application. Read the sidebars for additional insight to enrich the experience. Note the optional passage to memorize and determine if this discipline would be helpful for you. Do not allow yourself to be intimidated by women who have more time or who are gifted differently.

Make your Bible study—whatever level you choose—a top priority. Consider spacing your study throughout the week so that you can take time to ponder and meditate on what the Holy Spirit is teaching you. Do not make other appointments during the group Bible study. Ask God to enable you to attend faithfully. Come with an excitement to learn from others and a desire to share yourself and your journey. Give it your best, and remember that God promises to join you on this adventure that can change your life.

Why Study Ruth?

Recently, a young seminary student melted down in my office in a full-blown anxiety attack. I was concerned that she might pass out or throw up. I helped her to calm down, spent some time with her, and directed her to some quality counseling. She's not the first. In my Women Teaching Women course, students often tell their stories as part of their Bible teaching, and more and more I hear women sharing an unreasonable and uneasy sense of anxiety crippling them.

Research tells us that anxiety is spreading through society like a plague, especially in the younger generations. In 2018, the largest book retailer in the United States, Barnes and Noble, reported a huge surge in book sales on anxiety—a 25 percent jump in one year. Women are on more antianxiety meds than at any other time in history.

According to a 2018 *Medical News Today* article, "Anxiety in the West: Is It on the Rise?," richer countries report a higher prevalence of anxiety. Apparently when people feel less pressure to provide the basics, their thinking moves to other issues that are more difficult to control (Newman, "Anxiety in the West").

Another reason for this rise in anxiety is twenty-four-hour news coverage where we experience every tragedy and crisis in real time: political and racial turmoil, flesh-eating bacteria, antibiotic resistance, mass shootings, terrorism, and on and on. With all the craziness going on in our world today, worry has become a favorite pastime. It's often the favorite topic of conversation. Are you letting this craziness corrupt your spiritual, physical, and emotional health? Do you love someone who is? It's easy to do.

I'm certainly not immune. I grew up knowing nothing about God, and I battled severe depression and anxiety before Jesus found me. In my early years as a believer, I thought that worrying showed I was a caring Christian. I remember the day when our Bible study teacher taught us that worry and anxiety offend God, that they are signs we don't trust him. Ugh—convicting. As I've grown stronger in the Lord, I have learned that God does not want his daughters trapped in a crippling web of worry and anxiety.

First Pargraph reminded me of myself.

BREAK FREE FROM ANXIETY

But how do we break free from anxiety in our own lives and help others do the same? We must immerse ourselves in God's Word as a lifestyle—and not just a verse here and there. Our life goal must be to digest the Bible book by book as life-giving nourishment that cannot be attained any other way. We know that investing in a quality education makes us literate and alters our future. Many of us make sacrifices of years, money, and energy to educate ourselves because we understand education's benefits and rewards.

Biblical literacy is even more valuable! Over a span of sixteen hundred years, God orchestrated the creation of sixty-six documents written by the Holy Spirit through more than forty human authors who came from different backgrounds. Together they produced a unified love letter that communicates without error God's affection, grace, direction, truth, and wisdom. He did this so that we would not be left without access to his mind and heart (Hendricks and Hendricks, *Living by the Book*, 23).

THE INCREDIBLE BENEFITS OF BIBLICAL LITERACY

Earning a quality education changes us. An education in the Scriptures will change us even more. But just like with secular learning, becoming biblically literate requires a serious investment. However, the rewards and benefits far outweigh the increased lifetime earnings that come with a diploma from even the most prestigious Ivy League university. These are some of the benefits:

- an intimate relationship with the almighty God
- a true understanding of the way the world works and how to live well in it
- a supernatural ability to love ourselves and others
- insight into our own sin nature along with a path to overcome it, and if we fail, a way to wipe the shame slate clean, pick ourselves up forgiven, and move on with renewed hope
- meaning and purpose
- relational health lived in community
- support through struggles
- continued growth in becoming a person who exhibits the fruit of the Spirit: love, joy, peace, patience, kindness, goodness, faithfulness, gentleness, and self-control (Galatians 5:22–23)
- freedom from anxiety as we learn to trust in God's providential care

Every book of the Bible provides another layer in the scaffolding of truth that transforms our mind, heart, attitudes, and actions. As we work through this study in the book of Ruth, undoubtedly God will speak to each of us individually, applying the book's truths to our particular situations and needs. But one of the book's main purposes is to help us *all* learn to trust in God's providential care over us, resulting in freedom from anxiety.

IT'S *NOT* A HALLMARK MOVIE ROMANCE

If you've studied the book of Ruth before, perhaps you focused on the romance between Ruth and Boaz, the fidelity of Ruth to her mother-in-law, Naomi, or Naomi's bitterness redeemed. And those components deserve our attention, but they completely miss the main point of the book. The book of Ruth is no script for a Hallmark movie. Instead, the big idea of this book is God's tender care over women and their significant place in God's Big Story. Like a shepherd whose eye never leaves each individual sheep in his flock regardless of the challenges, God constantly protects his own—including the ewes.

BACKGROUND INFORMATION

The author of Ruth is unknown, but certainly whoever wrote this book experienced a deep look into the lives and emotions of the two main characters of the book—two women. The book was probably written during the reign of David or Solomon, when many women may have been asking, "Are the female sheep as valuable to God as the males? Does God truly care about women as much as men?"

I understand why women in Old Testament times might have asked that question since they lived in a society where women were second-class citizens, often bought and sold as property in arranged marriages, and financially helpless without a male provider. In these kinds of cultures, women yearn to know if God truly cares about them. Sadly, this "women are less than" attitude is still pervasive in some churches and cultures today, causing women to ask the same question. Does God truly care about women as much as men? This true story shouts a rip-roaring *yes!*

God is the hero of the book. He illustrates his providential care over Ruth and Naomi, evidenced by his guidance of their steps every day, even when situations looked bleak and hopeless. We can know through their lives that God truly leads and feeds women who love him, even when disasters strike, loved ones die, and the cupboard is bare. Not only does he protect and provide for them, but he also honors their fidelity and humility by preserving their story in his Word and by placing them, along with honorable men, in the lineage of the Messiah, the Son of God. Amazing!

Strap on your sandals and get ready to join me for a true faith-building adventure fraught with suspense, tragedy, excitement, and surprise.

The Vale of Tears | LESSON 1

I label the six years after I graduated college my "vale of tears." The term *vale* comes from a Middle English word that means a valley or dale. The term symbolizes a down time when everything goes wrong. During those six years, my father lost a four-year battle with stomach cancer, my mother reacted with rage and rejection, a seven-year romantic relationship ended in heartbreak, I mourned over losing my college friends, and I hated my job. I still recall those six years as a time of deep sadness and extreme anxiety. Have you experienced a "vale of tears"? Living in a fallen, broken world means all of us will sometimes walk through these kinds of valleys.

What thoughts invade your mind in the vale? When we are in these valleys and lose control, we can easily feel helpless and hopeless. Our thoughts can spiral from one worst-case scenario to another. Do you find yourself overcome with anxious thoughts? Do you find yourself anxious that more pain and more dark days are ahead?

Do you easily jump to the conclusion that God doesn't love you? Are you afraid these situations are the result of some sin in your life? Do you fear God is angry with you and he's punishing you? Do you feel abandoned, as if God neither knows nor cares about your pain? Although these are common responses, they reflect the reality that we really don't know God that well.

God preserved the book of Ruth to help us see deeply into his heart even in the saddest, most anxious times, to learn to trust him in the vale of tears, and to overcome fears that lead to an anxious lifestyle.

Read Ruth 1:1.

1. The book begins by telling us that this true account took place "when the judges ruled" (1:1). To truly understand any biblical story, we must learn about the kinds of things that were going on during that time period (1375–1050 BC). Generally what can you glean from the passages in Judges below? (Judges is the book before Ruth.) How did people treat one another? Envision yourself living in that culture.

Orthodox Jews read the book of Ruth annually at the Feast of Pentecost because the feast takes place during the harvest season that coincides with Ruth and Boaz's encounter and betrothal on the barley threshing floor.   —Sue

Elimelek is King

Naomi is main
Chart. not Ruth
moah - Eneny Tuesday

Judges 2:10–13

There arose another generation. the people did evil in sight of the lord abondoned the lord, the Gods of their fathers.
they went after other Gods, from among the Gods of the peoples were around them

19:22

When ever the judge died, they turned back & were more corrupt than their fathers, going after other Gods, Serving them + bowing down do them
they did not drop their stubborn orpractices. so the anger of the lord was Kindled
21:23
against Israel, drove out
He will no longer walk about before them — the lord left those nations not driving them out quickly and he did not give them into the hand of Joshua

21:25

2. How was the time of the judges similar to our "times" today?

In Irael's unfaithfulness

3. The time when the judges ruled was a downward spiral of a series of cycles—rebellion, retribution, repentance, and restoration—that evolved into centuries of greater and greater chaos. How do you think this kind of chaos was likely to affect the lives of people living during those times? How much more often would these people experience a "vale of tears"? Why?

The vale of tears, also known as the valley of tears, is a phrase that refers to a Christian doctrine that teaches that life's tribulations are a part of the human experience and won't end completely until one leaves this world and enters into the eternal state. The phrase appears in the English translation of the German Lutheran hymn "Be Still, My Soul," written in 1855, and comes from Psalm 84:6–7, where it says, "the Valley of Baka," meaning "the valley of weeping."   —Sue

🌼 Read Ruth 1:2–5.

4. We find the names and identities of the main characters in verses 2–5. Describe them and their relationships to one another.

Elimelek

Naomi

Mahlon

Kilion

Orpah

Ruth

Elimelek packed up his family and traveled to Moab hoping to find work
to support his wife and two sons. Moab is the historical name for a moun-
tainous region in what is now Jordan. The trek would have taken an
exhausting seven to ten days and required them to cross the river Jordan
and navigate various kinds of terrain.

5. Naomi could easily have felt anxious when moving into Moabite territory where Israelites were unwelcome. Have you ever relocated to a new city or country that forced you to make various adjustments? If so, what emotions accompanied those adjustments? How long, if ever, did it take for you to feel completely at home?

6. Elimelek's family were outsiders in Moab, and later in our story Ruth experienced being an outsider in Bethlehem. Have you ever felt like an "outsider"? Describe that experience below and consider sharing with the group.

The tribe of Moab originated as descendants of Lot and the sexual relations he shared with his two daughters (Gen. 19:30–38). Incestuous beginnings for the Moabite tribe resulted in bad blood between them and the Israelites.
—Marnie Legaspi ("Ruth: The So-Called Scandal," 61)

DIGGING DEEPER

For more insight into the origins of the Moabites, study Genesis 19:30–38. What do you learn about the beginning of this ancient tribe?

During the families' ten-year stay in Moab, they experienced loss after loss.

7. Describe the first loss in 1:3. How would this loss have affected the family?

Should we interpret all the losses of Elimelek's family as God's judgment for failing to trust him when they moved to Moab? Scholars disagree, but Robert Chisholm Jr., chair and senior professor of Old Testament Studies at Dallas Theological Seminary writes, "The tragic deaths of Elimelech and his sons should not be interpreted as acts of divine judgment because there is not enough evidence in the immediate context or in the broader context of the Old Testament to sustain such a theory. On the contrary, it would seem that their deaths, like the famine and their move to Moab, are incidental details that set the stage for the story to follow" (*A Commentary on Judges and Ruth*, 599).   —Sue

8. Have you ever walked in the shoes of a widow or walked with a widow through her grief? What are some of the emotions you've experienced or observed?

9. Naomi also became a single parent the day Elimelek died. Have you ever walked in the shoes of a single mother or walked with a single mother through her challenges? What emotions did you experience or observe?

10. How do you think losing their father might have affected Naomi's two sons?

11. What did the two sons do to deal with their new family situation (1:4)? Can you think of reasons why they might have taken this action? What were they hoping for?

12. Instead of their situation improving, things got worse. What losses darkened the lives of these women even more (1:5)?

DIGGING DEEPER

Some scholars label Naomi the Bible's female Job. Digest Job 1 and compare his circumstances with the situations Naomi and her two daughters-in-law encounter. How did Job initially respond? How did he respond later in his story as his trials increased (Job 6:1–4; 13:20–27; 23:1–7; 42:1–6)?

13. Have you or someone you love struggled with infertility? If you are comfortable, share the experience and what infertility probably meant for Ruth and Orpah.

14. What losses have you experienced in your life? What were your thoughts about God during these difficult times?

15. What helped you move through these losses? What did you learn?

16. What has Lesson 1 taught you about the realities of life? What are you hoping to learn as we continue in our adventure with Naomi and Ruth?

Cast all your anxiety on him because he cares for you.
—1 Peter 5:7

The narrative finds itself right in the middle of the cyclical pattern of sin, suffering, supplication, and salvation found in Judges. But this story stands as a ray of light, showing the power of God's great loving-kindness (Hebrew chesed; *Ruth 1:8) for His faithful people. The author gives the reader a snapshot perspective—focusing on one family in a small town—as opposed to the broader narrative found in Judges.*

CHARLES SWINDOLL (*Swindoll Study Bible*, 321)

In five short verses, death wipes the men off the scene, leaving three grieving widows behind. In a male-centered culture that ascribed value to women based on their relationships to men, these husbandless, sonless women hold no interest to anyone. In many minds . . . the story is over. Nothing is left to tell. Yet ironically, this is where the narrative heats up as the biblical spotlight settles on Naomi and an all-female cast. Now the real story begins.
—Carolyn Custis James
(*Gospel of Ruth*, 33)

The Long Walk Home | LESSON 2

It's normal to feel concerned waiting on the results of a second mammogram, before an important job interview, or carrying a screaming child out of a grocery store. It's normal to feel grieved when tragedy strikes. But if those emotions become unwarranted, unreasonable, or uncontrollable, we have moved into unhealthy anxiety. God doesn't want his daughters trapped in a web of anxious feelings. That's where we find Naomi.

My earnest hope is that I would weather Naomi's devastating circumstances with stalwart faith, amazing everyone around me. But the truth is, I don't know. Sometimes I'm so strong in trusting God that I surprise myself. Sometimes I buckle under due to situations that I know I should be able to handle better. I find it's the scaffolding of one trial on top of another for long periods of time that wears me down, and then I disappoint myself.

But I've learned that God doesn't condemn me when I fail. He understands my need to process through my pain in healthy ways. He's taught me to run to him with those feelings and to work through them with healthy people who know and love me well. God knows that we are merely dust and that as humans we sometimes fall. What do we do when we are down, and how do we prepare for those times? None of us knows for sure how we will respond if God asks us to walk through the kinds of trials that Naomi and Job experienced. The best we can do is consistently invest in our relationship with God, knowing he will make a way through the heartache and enable us to get up again. Do you want to keep anxiety from overtaking your life? Give God your best as we journey together through the book of Ruth.

 Read Ruth 1:6–22.

(How many references to God can you find in these verses? _____)

1. What news prompted Naomi to consider returning to her hometown, Bethlehem in Israel (1:6)? How does Naomi interpret this news? What does this reveal about her?

2. What preparations do you think the three women needed to make for this move?

3. Soon after they set out on their journey, Naomi had a change of heart concerning her daughters-in-law. Envision her stopping somewhere along the road, finding a place to rest, and sitting face-to-face to engage with them. She begins the conversation with an order and two blessings (1:8–9):

   The order

The first blessing

The second blessing

What do you learn about their relationships from these words?

When Naomi bestows her first blessing, she says, "May the LORD show you kindness, as you have shown kindness to your dead husbands and to me" (1:8). The word for kindness here is the Hebrew word *hesed*, and we'll see it throughout our study. It's not easy to translate because no English equivalent exists. It's a combination of loyalty and loving-kindness. Maybe loyal love comes closest. It's the way God loves people and the way he wants them to love one another. It's the outworking of the emotion of loyal love that results in the deepest and richest kind of sacrificial love in action that we can experience. We observe *hesed* in thriving long-term marriages and devoted parental love for beloved children, but nowhere is *hesed* better illustrated than in the sacrifice that Jesus made on the cross for us.   —Sue

4. Naomi wished that her daughters–in–law would experience the same kind of loyal love they had given her and her sons. When you think of the word *hesed* (see sidebar), does someone you know come to mind? What makes them a living illustration of this beautiful word?

5. Ruth and Orpah both faced life-altering choices that day. Would they take the road forward or the road back? What choice do you think you would have made and why? What criteria do you often use to determine significant choices in your life?

6. How does anxiety affect your decision-making ability? How would you advise a friend who needs to make a life-altering choice in the midst of anxiety?

7. Envision the scene in 1:9–13.

What did Ruth and Orpah do and say when Naomi kissed them goodbye?

Why did Naomi argue that Ruth and Orpah would be better off staying in Moab?

Without some insight into the radical differences in their culture and ours, it's difficult for any of us to understand Naomi's arguments. Consider the following unquestioned norms of many of the ancient Near Eastern cultures of the Bible:

- The concept of "romantic" love and individualism were not highly valued. Thriving depended upon strong family units continuing for many generations. Families earned their living together on farms or in small shops, requiring everyone to do their part.
- As soon as girls showed promise of childbearing, their family typically arranged a marriage, often to an older man, that would benefit the family unit. Unmarried women had no way to support themselves and only in the home of a father or husband could a woman be sure of respect and protection.

DIGGING DEEPER

To learn more about ancient customs that affect how we interpret passages related to women in the Bible, read: *Women in the World of the Earliest Christians: Illuminating Ancient Ways of Life* by Lynn H. Cohick and *Vindicating the Vixens: Revisiting Sexualized, Vilified, and Marginalized Women of the Bible* edited by Sandra Glahn.

- Generally, adult life spans were much shorter than today, and infant mortality rates were much higher. As a result a healthy woman who could bear many children was highly prized by the family.
- Widowhood, even for young women, was much more common than today, and widows without a family's care lived in danger and insecurity. Knowing these dangers, God gave women protection in the Old Testament Mosaic law in Deuteronomy 25:5–6 in a practice known as levirate marriage:

> If brothers are living together and one of them dies without a son, his widow must not marry outside the family. Her husband's brother shall take her and marry her and fulfill the duty of a brother-in-law to her. The first son she bears shall carry on the name of the dead brother so that his name will not be blotted out from Israel.

Naomi's advice to her daughters-in-law in 1:11–13 makes more sense when we understand this practice designed to protect women. The obligatory custom of levirate marriage will play an even more important role later in our story.

Please don't assume that God approves of all these customs regarding women. This simply was the way it was, and we can't gain a clear understanding of what's going on and what God wants us to learn unless we are aware of the world they were navigating.

DIGGING DEEPER

Compare Naomi's words in 1:13 with Job's statements in Job 16:12–13 and 27:2. What do these two important biblical figures have in common? What can we learn from their experiences?

8. What can you learn about Naomi's emotional state at this moment from 1:13?

9. Do you think Naomi's statement, "It is more bitter for me than for you, because the LORD's hand has turned against me!" was true? In what sense did Naomi's prospects for a better life seem more hopeless than her daughters-in-law? In what sense was Naomi's statement false?

> Naomi's words seem to have their greatest effect on her. It is as if by verbalizing the awful truth about the death of her own hopes that the painful reality of her losses sinks in with renewed force. It is a Job moment, when she can no longer stifle what her sufferings imply about God.
> —Carolyn Custis James
> (*Gospel of Ruth*, 46–47)

10. Put yourself in Naomi's sandals. For example, imagine you are in your senior years, you outlived your husband and all your children, and your entire retirement fund was lost in an investment gone wrong, taking your home and car with it. How do you think you would respond if everything that happened to Naomi in Moab happened to you?

11. What was your honest first reaction to Naomi's declaration of bitterness in 1:13? Did you battle a critical spirit? Or did you feel compassion, concern, or some other emotion? What's your typical first reaction toward Christians who express bitterness in the midst of difficult circumstances?

12. In the midst of more tears, Orpah gives in to Naomi's pleadings and walks away. What does Ruth do instead (1:14)? What does Ruth's body language communicate to Naomi?

13. What do you learn about loyal love from Ruth's *hesed* declaration in 1:16–17?

Where you go I will go, and where you stay I will stay.

Your people will be my people and your God my God.

Where you die I will die, and there I will be buried.

May the LORD deal with me, be it ever so severely, if even death separates you and me.

14. Ruth's declaration has been used in marriage vows for centuries. But what are some ways that *hesed*, God's loyal love, can be lived out in other relationships besides marriage?

15. Has anyone ever loved you with *hesed*, God's loyal love? Have you ever loved someone that way? How might *hesed* change the course of someone's life?

16. How might someone's expression of *hesed* help another person overcome toxic anxiety? Have you ever experienced this on the giving or receiving end?

Scripture's introduction to Bethlehem isn't pretty. Jacob buried his favorite wife, Rachel, on the way to Bethlehem after she died a tragic death (Gen. 35:16–19). The book of Judges mentions Bethlehem in conjunction with a corrupt priest who became a mercenary for idolaters (Judg. 17:7–9). Another account describes a concubine from Bethlehem who was brutally raped and dismembered (Judg. 19:1–30). Not a great beginning for the little town of Bethlehem.
—Charles Swindoll
(*Swindoll Study Bible*, 324)

17. Realizing Ruth's determination, Naomi succumbs and makes the seven- to ten-day walk to Bethlehem with her. What happened when they arrived? What did the townswomen say as they gathered around them to welcome Naomi home? (1:19)

18. How might intense grief and more than ten years' separation change someone's appearance?

19. What does Naomi tell the townswomen as she shares about her time in Moab (1:20–21)? How might processing her grief with these friends help her in the future? (Be on the lookout to see if her attitude changes as we continue in her adventure.)

20. How do you process your emotions when you are sad, disappointed, or devastated?

Barley served as a grain staple in the Hebrew diet, used in breads and cereals. The Israelites grew their own food, and their economy depended on successful harvests, making the harvests very significant events. They had three a year: the barley harvest came in April and May, the wheat harvest came about six weeks later in June and July, and the ingathering of fruit occurred in September and October. —Sue

Workers reaped the barley with sickles, tied the stalks in bunches (sheaves), and transported them to the threshing floor. To remove the barley grain from the stalks, workers would beat the sheaves with a rod or oxen would trample the stalks. Threshing floors were outdoors where the clay soil could be packed down into a hard surface. —Sue

Israeli towns were tight-knit, highly relational communities. We aren't told exactly how Naomi and Ruth provided a roof over their heads initially. Irving Jensen suggests that when Naomi returned from Moab, she may have sold her husband's land to provide temporary shelter for herself and Ruth. However, losing the land came at a high price because the land was the next generation's inheritance. With no prospects of a future son to carry on the family name and inherit the land, the family line and Elimelek's name would disappear forever. In this culture, this amounted to paramount tragedy. If someone in Naomi's extended family did not buy back, or redeem, the land, all hope for the continuation of the family would be lost. Naomi mourned not only for herself but also for the loss of her family's identity and future (*Judges and Ruth*, 89).

21. The author makes a point of telling us that Naomi and Ruth arrived in Bethlehem just as the barley harvest was beginning. What do you know about the concept of "harvest" in the Bible that might imply some positive foreshadowing in our adventure?

The atmosphere of simple piety that pervades the story, the sense throughout of an overruling providence, and the setting in that quiet corner of Judah all conspire to remind us that the story comes straight from the heart of that Hebrew consciousness of divine destiny which was later to reach so glorious a fulfillment.
G. T. MANLEY (*The New Bible Handbook*, 166)

The Harvest | LESSON 3

OPTIONAL

Memorize Psalm 91:3–4
Surely he [God] will save you from the fowler's snare and from the deadly pestilence. He will cover you with his feathers, and under his wings you will find refuge; his faithfulness will be your shield and rampart.

*Anxiety is a thin stream of fear trickling through the mind.
If encouraged, it cuts a channel into which all other
thoughts are drained.*
—Arthur Somers Roche

What's your initial reaction when you realize you are allowing anxiety to consume you? We can choose whether to "encourage" that thin stream of fear or to dam it up. If we give fear free rein, it will dig a deep channel through our minds and hearts until it drowns out everything else we think and feel. With all the loss and tragedy in their lives, certainly Naomi and Ruth battled anxiety, but only one succumbed to the flood of feelings that can so easily carry us away. Learn how to overcome anxiety from these two weary widows.

The new arrivals' celebrity status has worn off, and Naomi and Ruth are faced with providing a roof over their heads and enough food to stave off starvation. Some scholars believe Naomi may have sold the land that belonged to her husband's family, their most precious possession and inheritance for their offspring, in order to meet their basic needs for a while. But without land to grow their own food or family to help, they soon realize the cupboard is bare.

Intrepid Ruth has been learning all she can about the customs of her new community and faith. She finds that God has made provision for women like herself in the Mosaic law:

Do not deprive the foreigner or the fatherless of justice, or take the cloak of the widow as a pledge. Remember that you were slaves in Egypt and the LORD your God redeemed you from there. That is why I command you to do this. When you are harvesting in your field and you overlook a sheaf, do not go back to get it. Leave it for the foreigner, the fatherless and the widow, so that the LORD your God may bless you in all the work of your hands. (Deuteronomy 24:17–19)

 **Read Ruth 2:1–18.**

1. From what you now know about the needs of women in the ancient biblical world, why do you think the author introduced this section with the information in verse 1?

DIGGING DEEPER

From the following verses, what can you glean about God's heart for widows (Exodus 22:22–24; Deuteronomy 10:18; Psalm 68:5–6; 146:9; Isaiah 1:17)?

2. What does the author want us to know about this person from verse 1?

3. Concerned about their empty cupboard, what does Ruth suggest? How does Naomi respond, and what does Naomi call Ruth? (2:2)

4. Have you ever experienced an empty cupboard or other extreme financial trials? If so, help the group understand what Naomi and Ruth might be feeling. What helped?

5. What difference is Ruth's presence making in Naomi's life now? Has someone befriended you at a critical time in your life? Have you befriended someone else? What difference can even the presence of another person make if we are suffering alone and feeling desperate? Is God asking you to walk alongside someone who needs you right now?

Much is made of Naomi and Ruth in a mother-daughter relationship. But it is friendship that most characterizes their bond. Both widowed, they understand grief, but also significant in their enduring kinship is the experience of being an alien in a foreign, and sometimes unfriendly, land. They had each other, and that union proved as strong as marriage or motherhood.
—Ruth Tucker (*Dynamic Women of the Bible*, 133)

6. Ruth walked out of town into the barley fields around Bethlehem, chose a field in which to glean, and began to pick up the sheaves behind the hired workers. What does the author want you to know about her choice (2:3)? Why is her choice significant?

7. Have you ever made a "random" choice only to find out later that God was working through that selection for his specific purposes? If so, share the experience with the group. What did you learn about God?

8. In the afternoon, Boaz, the owner of that field, arrived. How did he greet his workers and how did they respond (2:4)? What does this interaction reveal about their character and relationship?

9. Boaz noticed Ruth and questioned the overseer about her identity (2:5–7). What do you learn about Ruth from the overseer's response?

10. Later Boaz struck up a conversation with Ruth (2:8–13).

How did Boaz address her (2:8)? What does that suggest concerning their age difference?

What were Boaz's bold initial instructions?

What provisions had Boaz already made for her safety? What does this reveal concerning his character?

Probably overwhelmed with gratitude, what does Ruth do and say in 2:10? What does this reveal about her character?

What did Boaz already know about Ruth's story (2:11)?

DIGGING DEEPER

When Boaz pronounced a blessing on Ruth in 2:12, he concludes with an analogy found in Psalm 91:4. What's the analogy and what do you learn about Boaz from the words he says over her?

In verse 12, Boaz pronounces a blessing upon Ruth. What does he hope for her?

How does this conversation with Boaz affect Ruth? What is her hope? (2:13)

11. What character qualities are evident in the men you most admire? Are you attracted to men with admirable qualities or other kinds of men? Discern why, if you can.

12. How did Ruth's first day gleaning in Boaz's barley field conclude (2:14–18)?

Scholars disagree on the weight of an "ephah" of barley, but it may have been as much as thirty pounds. Whatever the exact amount, Naomi expressed astonishment at Boaz's generosity and saw this as God's providential care over them. —Sue

 Read Ruth 2:19–23.

Ruth returned home to Naomi with her satchel running over with barley and roasted grain.

13. Envision the look on Naomi's face and her voice when she questioned Ruth about her day. Can you recall a time when you received some joyful, life-altering news? What happened and how did you feel?

Light in a messenger's eyes brings joy to the heart, and good news gives health to the bones.
—Proverbs 15:30

14. What did Naomi tell Ruth about Boaz in 2:20?

15. Naomi used the word *kindness*, the Hebrew word *hesed*, to describe Boaz in 2:20. Recall the meaning of this word from Lesson 1 or see the sidebar to refresh your memory. What does this word reveal about Boaz's motives in befriending Ruth and Naomi?

Naomi explained to Ruth that Boaz was their "guardian-redeemer" or "kinsman-redeemer." In order to fully understand why this is so important to the story, we must familiarize ourselves with the meaning of this legal term in the Mosaic law. Leviticus 25:25 commands, "If one of your fellow Israelites becomes poor and sells some of their property, their nearest relative is to come and redeem what they have sold."

God designated this person as the guardian of the extended family's interests, the one to provide and care for them, particularly the vulnerable. Thriving and even surviving in these hostile conditions required that the family unit take responsibility for one another, especially for women in a culture that deferred to men. While Ruth gleaned in the fields, Naomi probably spent hours on her knees in constant prayer, asking God to help them, two powerless widows. No doubt, Ruth's report from the field sparked hope that God had not forgotten them after all.

16. What do you think was Naomi's secret hope as she watched these circumstances unfold? As a result of that hope, what were her instructions for Ruth (2:22)?

17. Have you had a time in your life when you recovered from a "bitter spirit" or a series of discouraging events? What helped you regain your spiritual, emotional, and mental health?

18. The author informs us in 2:23 that Ruth gleaned in Boaz's fields through the barley and wheat harvests, from late March through late May. In light of the first day's interaction between Ruth, Boaz, and the other workers described in 2:4–16, what relational connections do you surmise may have transacted during those two months?

19. Often the relationship between Ruth and Boaz is romanticized as if it were a twenty-first century Hallmark movie. From what you have observed so far in our study, do you think their relationship is the point of the story for us? Or do you think there is something else God wants to teach us through their story? Who do you think will be the real hero of the story: Naomi, Ruth, Boaz, or God? Why?

It has been said that what we are determines what we see. We may look for God and miss Him because we confuse Him with shining angels. God is found not just in the miraculous . . . He is at work in us and through us in the dailiness of life. On a dreary Tuesday afternoon we can get the idea that life is all up to us. But if we belong to God, even when we don't see Him at work, we can be sure that God is moving events on our behalf.
ALICE MATHEWS (*A Woman God Can Lead*, 78)

The Ask | LESSON 4

For somehow, not only for Christmas, but all the long year through,
The joy that you give to others is the joy that comes back to you;
And the more you spend in blessing the poor, the lonely and sad,
The more to your heart's possessing, returns to make you glad.
—Margaret Sangster, "The Christmas Tree"

OPTIONAL

Memorize Habakkuk 3:17–19
Though the fig tree does not bud and there are no grapes on the vines, though the olive crop fails and the fields produce no food, though there are no sheep in the pen and no cattle in the stalls, yet I will rejoice in the LORD, I will be joyful in God my Savior. The Sovereign LORD is my strength; he makes my feet like the feet of a deer, he enables me to tread on the heights.

My best defense against anxiety is to lift the focus off myself and direct it to someone else who needs help. Naomi found the same principle true for herself, and you'll find it true as well.

In the months since she and Ruth arrived, Naomi has experienced hints of God's providential care, proving that he has not abandoned her. Encouraged, she turns her thoughts to Ruth's welfare. She realizes it's likely Ruth will outlive Naomi. No jobs exist for widows to provide for themselves. Without inclusion in a family unit, Ruth's prospects look bleak. But how can she secure Ruth's future? In Bethlehem, men negotiate marriages, usually involving a dowry and social connections. Ruth has neither and no man to speak for her. Nevertheless, Naomi concocts a bold and somewhat dangerous plan.

Read Ruth 3:1–7.

Envision Naomi and Ruth nestled in their little abode when Naomi strikes up a conversation and shares her plan with Ruth. Naomi knows that Boaz will be spending the night on the threshing floor to protect his barley harvest from thieves (1 Samuel 23:1). She gives Ruth strange and specific orders (Ruth 3:3–4).

1. How is Ruth to prepare for this "adventure" (3:3)? It's likely Ruth is still wearing the traditional attire of a widow. What is Naomi symbolically asking of Ruth?

2. What did Naomi tell Ruth to do when she arrived at the threshing floor (3:3)?

3. What did Naomi tell her to do as darkness set in (3:4)?

4. What potential dangers concern you as Ruth acts on Naomi's plan? What does Naomi know that she believes will keep Ruth safe?

5. Have you ever chosen to place yourself in danger for a worthy cause? If so, share your experience with the group. What did you learn?

 Read Ruth 3:8–13.

6. Ruth followed Naomi's orders carefully. What would be your emotional state if you had been Ruth lying at the feet of Boaz in the middle of the night?

7. Startled, Boaz awakened in the dim moonlight, probably threw off his blanket, recognized that there was a woman at his feet, and exclaimed, "Who are you?" How did Ruth answer him (3:9)? Recall the first blessing Boaz gave Ruth in 2:12. What was the hidden message in her words?

About now in our adventure, we must each decide whether or not the scene on the threshing floor is really more about *hesed* or testosterone. Many male scholars in the past chose the latter, but I'm inclined to go with the former. The latter sexualizes the book and makes marriage and men the answer to every woman's problems. Although I've been happily married for forty-seven years to a good man I adore, I loved raising my kids, and I thoroughly enjoy my five "above average" grandkids, I don't believe that's the big idea of the book. What determines a woman's value in God's eyes? Not all women choose to marry, and the Bible says their choice is honorable (1 Corinthians 7). Not all women can bear children, yet a gracious God doesn't determine their value by their motherhood status. It's good for a woman to invest in a family and to walk through life with an appropriate husband, but it's just as good to serve God solo on the mission field, in ministry, or in some other respected endeavor. Top priority for all of us is our relationship with God. So if the big idea of the book isn't teaching women that they must find their value in marriage or motherhood, what is?   —Sue

8. Boaz responded by blessing Ruth and addressing her again as "daughter." What compliments did Boaz pay Ruth in 3:10–11 that showed he'd been observing her character since she arrived in Bethlehem?

Neither Boaz nor the nearer relative was required to step in and help Naomi and Ruth according to levirate law because neither was Elimelek's biological "brother." But Boaz saw their dire situation and was willing to step in and help even though not required by law.   —Sue

9. Boaz was willing to step into the role of guardian-redeemer for Ruth and Naomi, but what obstacle stood in the way (3:12)?

DIGGING DEEPER

Another woman in the Bible also needed the protection that the levirate marriage law provided. Her name was Tamar and we find her story in Genesis 38. What happened to Tamar that illustrates the contrast between Judah and Boaz?

10. What was Boaz's attitude about the situation with the closer relative (3:13)? What does this reveal about his character?

11. What does this whole episode on the threshing floor reveal about the nature of godly men?

12. What qualities do you honestly value in men? What cultural factors do you think influence your ideas about men? (For example, our hyper-sexual culture's expectations of men? Radical feminist views about men? People who insist that differences between men and women don't exist?) Discuss graciously.

13. Can you think of any nonbiblical ideas about men that some churches promote? How might these ideas harm healthy marriages and men and women working together in ministry?

14. Who do you know that you would praise as a godly man? Why? Give specific examples that lead you to this conclusion.

 Read Ruth 3:14–18.

15. Boaz instructed Ruth to lie at his feet until morning instead of making her way home then (3:14). What do you think might have been his motivation?

16. What did Boaz do as Ruth was preparing to walk home as the sun rose (3:15)? What was he communicating to her through this action?

17. When Ruth arrived home, she reported everything to Naomi. (By the way, these are Ruth's last words in the book.) What was Naomi's response (3:18)?

18. How do you think Naomi and Ruth felt as they waited for the settling of the matter? Can you recall a time when you were forced to wait for a life-altering event or decision? How did you wait? If you have learned to wait well, share your insight with the group.

What now happens at the threshing floor is as essential to the story-teller's purpose as what happened on the Moabite highway between Ruth and Naomi, or what happened in the harvest scene when Boaz praised an impoverished widow who was gleaning, or what will happen in the solemn civil hearing at the city gate. At each of these points in the story, a moment of choice is presented to both actors and audience, and at each of these points the choice is made in favor of what righteous living calls for.
EDWARD CAMPBELL JR. (*Ruth*, 132)

The Obstacle | LESSON 5

Godly men stepped forward and opened significant doors for me, and not just heavy physical doors, but doors of opportunity to serve the Lord. They've championed me, giving me places to excel that were formerly not open to women. They voluntarily used their power and influence on my behalf, and I'll be eternally grateful. Jesus was like that, and so was Boaz.

Consider for a moment the irony in our adventure. Boaz wields significant power as a man, an influential leader in his clan, and a wealthy businessman in the community. Ruth and Naomi, two childless widows, occupy the lowest rung on the social ladder. Our story this week begins with an unexpected twist.

> Instead of firmly reminding [Ruth] of the way things are sup-
> posed to work, [Boaz is] up the next morning before the crack
> of dawn, shredding his to-do list and notifying his assistant to
> cancel all engagements for the day. A busy man . . . is dropping
> everything and heading into town on a mission Ruth and her
> mother-in-law cooked up. . . . They are hardly the kind of VIPs
> for whom a man suspends his business engagements for the day.
> What is happening to Boaz? (Custis James, *Gospel of Ruth*, 176)

❧ Read Ruth 4:1–12.

The next part of the saga causes most of us to shake our heads in confusion. It's difficult for modern-day westerners to understand what's going on unless we grasp the complicated legal processes that governed Old Testament Hebrew communities. God designed particular laws to help families thrive and to protect the vulnerable. These laws are completely foreign to our western way of thinking, but they had their purpose in those cultures. I'll offer some insight as we proceed to provide a general understanding of the day's legal procedures. Keep in mind that what's most important is to generally digest how these proceedings at the town gate lead to God's desired outcomes.

This life-altering day begins with Boaz gathering the involved parties at the town gate—himself, the anonymous other guardian-redeemer, and ten elders to make up the needed legal quorum (4:1–2).

1. Like a skilled lawyer, Boaz begins by laying out the legal matter that needed resolving. What situation has brought them together (4:3)? See the sidebar for clarification.

2. Have you ever found yourself entangled in a complex legal situation? What emotions did you experience? Why are these circumstances often so scary?

3. What does Boaz suggest to the closer relative and what's his response? Who is next in line to take on this legal responsibility if the closer relative declines? (4:4)

4. Boaz informs the relative that if he acquires Elimelek's land, according to the spirit of the levirate marriage law, he will also need to marry Ruth and attempt to produce an heir with her. That son will take the place of Elimelek's heir and will inherit the family property and carry on Elimelek's name (4:5). What's the relative's response now and why (4:6)?

5. From the book of Ruth we observe the value that culture and community placed on family in biblical times. Do you enjoy a supportive family? If so, share some of the benefits. If not, what provision has God made for those who cannot claim that blessing?

Boaz argues that morally, family must take care of family. Their relative Elimelek's land may be sold to someone outside the family, and Elimelek has no living sons to carry on his name. As a result, his name may be lost forever. The family must step in and do something in the spirit of levirate marriage as well as Leviticus 25:35: "If any of your fellow Israelites becomes poor and are unable to support themselves among you, help them as you would a foreigner and stranger, so they can continue to live among you."

As we saw, these Mosaic laws addressed Ruth's situation: her husband died without an heir and, under the law, the "brother" was required to marry and sire a child through his widow. That son would take on the husband's name and inherit the husband's property. Although neither the nearer relative nor Boaz were the "brother," the spirit of the law suggested that family provide for family.

Aren't you grateful that we no longer live under the Mosaic law? Because of Jesus, we live in an era of grace. However, God designed these laws for ancient cultures to help the people thrive and to protect the vulnerable, especially women. God calls us to live out the spirit of those laws voluntarily today.

Why did the nearer relative decline? According to Carolyn Custis James: "Both laws [the levirate law and the kinsman-redeemer law] were costly and involved enormous sacrifice. Since a father's estate was divided among his sons, when one son died childless, the surviving brothers' inheritance automatically increased. . . . The brother whose duty it was to marry the widow was spoiling his own inheritance if he succeeded in fathering a son by her. . . . According to these calculations, becoming your brother's keeper is a losing proposition. But it is the *hesed*-way of doing things" (*Gospel of Ruth*, 149–50).

6. If you found yourself at the town gate dealing with this kind of situation, do you think you would respond more like the closer relative or more like Boaz? Why?

7. How might you apply the spirit of the levirate marriage and the guardian-redeemer laws to your life today?

To seal the legal transaction, the closer relative removed his sandal and gave it to Boaz. Scholars aren't sure of the origin of this practice although it may be derived from an ancient Egyptian custom. The owner had walked upon his land in this sandal, and in giving the sandal to the new owner, he was acknowledging the buyer's right to walk on the land he now owned.

8. Boaz pronounced a legal summary of the dealings in 4:9–10. What is he promising to do and what are the hoped-for results?

> All God sets out to do, He does. All He has ever been, He is. His will cannot be frustrated. His church cannot be crushed. His Word cannot pass away. His promises cannot fail. His plans cannot be thwarted, His power cannot be resisted.
> —John Bisagno (*God Is*, 16)

9. What will this life-altering event mean for Naomi?

10. What was the general attitude of the elders and the community who witnessed these proceedings (4:11–12)? What does their response tell us about the faith and values of the people of Bethlehem?

> Do you not know? Have you not heard? The LORD is the everlasting God, the Creator of the ends of the earth. He will not grow tired or weary, and his understanding no one can fathom. He gives strength to the weary and increases the power of the weak. Even youths grow tired and weary, and young men stumble and fall; but those who hope in the LORD will renew their strength. They will soar on wings like eagles; they will run and not grow weary, they will walk and not be faint.
> —Isaiah 40:28–31

The Israelites knew their history and drew strength from that knowledge. To fully grasp the blessings the community pronounced upon Boaz, we must explore the people and places they included in their blessing. Let's look at each component of the blessing separately.

DIGGING DEEPER

What can you learn about the lives of Rachel and Leah from Genesis 29:16–35; 30:1–23; 31:19, 32–35; 35:16–26; and 46:19–22? Paint a word picture of how Ruth might relate to each sister.

11. "May the LORD make the woman who is coming into your home like Rachel and Leah, who together built up the family of Israel" (4:11). What blessing on Ruth can you deduce from verse 11?

12. "May you have standing in Ephrathah and be famous in Bethlehem" (4:11). What were the townsfolk hoping for Boaz? How is this blessing connected to Micah 5:2? (Stay tuned for God's amazing way of fulfilling this blessing in the next lesson.)

DIGGING DEEPER

For the whole story of the scandalous conception of Perez and the parallels between his mother Tamar and Ruth, study Genesis 38.

13. "Through the offspring the LORD gives you by this young woman, may your family be like that of Perez, whom Tamar bore to Judah" (4:12). Perez was a name everyone knew in Bethlehem because Elimelek, Boaz, the closer relative, and others in their extended family were all descended from him. Take a quick look at Ruth 4:18–22. What was the community hoping for Boaz?

14. That eventful day changed everything in Naomi's and Ruth's lives. Can you recall a time when your life changed dramatically because of an event or decision out of your control that was orchestrated by someone who showed you *hesed*? What happened and what difference did this time make in your life long-term? Looking back, if you see God's hands orchestrating circumstances that brought about this event, share it with the group.

We are destined for something more and better than to build the good life for ourselves. We were created to be like Jesus, and we can't be like him if we leave out submission. Like hesed, submission is another of God's great power tools for changing human lives, renovating this fallen planet, and putting our world to rights. . . . One wonders how different our world would be— how changed the evening news, how sharply abuse and violence statistics would decline, and how our relationships with one another would be enriched—if God's people truly heeded the call to the kind of submission Jesus advocates and we got serious about looking out for others. This is how Jesus works through us to bring wholeness to our broken world.
CAROLYN CUSTIS JAMES (*Gospel of Ruth*, 168–69)

The Serendipities

In 1981, pediatrician Michael Shannon saved the life of a 3.2-pound baby boy by working around the clock to stabilize him. In 2011, a semi-truck T-boned Dr. Shannon's SUV, pinning it under the truck where it caught fire. The Orange County paramedic, Chris Tokey, who rescued him, turned out to be the grown-up baby boy that Dr. Shannon had saved thirty years earlier (Chambers and Bloom, "OC Paramedic"). A coincidence or a divine encounter?

Life is full of serendipities, surprises from the hand of a Sovereign God, as we'll observe in the last leg of our journey with Naomi, Ruth, and Boaz. Our adventure began with the saga of Naomi and her family, and it ends the same way. The last we heard from Ruth was back in 3:18 as she waits for the results of Boaz's day at the town gate. We have no indication that Naomi and Ruth are even there. So much for our Hallmark romance.

It's likely that Boaz was quite a bit older than Ruth; only older men had earned the kind of respect the community gave Boaz as a leader. We aren't told anything about either one's physical attractiveness. Any romantic tension between them we likely dreamed up ourselves. And, as much as we are nauseated at the thought, Boaz probably had other wives and other children. To gain the prestige and stature Boaz enjoyed, he likely would have already been blessed with his own sons—to the community, a sign of God's favor. Only as we enter their world can we glean the universal truths that God wants us to see. Because although the culture and customs were radically different from ours, God's attributes and general workings in the world remain the same, but we can easily miss them if we attempt to lift their story out of context and plop it into a twenty-first century Hallmark scene.

Actually it's God who is the hero of their story, just as he is the hero of yours and mine. Come with me to the final act where we discover what God's been up to behind the scenes. Discover and worship.

 Read Ruth 4:13–22.

OPTIONAL

Memorize Romans 15:13

May the God of hope fill you with all joy and peace as you trust in him, so that you may overflow with hope by the power of the Holy Spirit.

1. Ruth and Boaz's wedding scene and their son's birth take all of one verse in the story (4:13). However, why is the birth a special reason to praise God?

2. Who are the characters in the final scene of our true drama (4:13–17)? Why do you think the author features Naomi instead of Ruth and Boaz?

3. The townswomen rejoice with Naomi. Who did they praise specifically (4:14)?

4. What did they say about Boaz?

5. Consider Boaz as a Christ figure. In what ways do Boaz's actions toward Ruth illustrate the work of Jesus in your life and mine?

6. What did the townspeople say about Ruth?

To the faithful you show yourself faithful.
—Psalm 18:25

7. In what ways did Ruth, and even ultimately Naomi, illustrate qualities of Jesus that we should emulate?

8. What part does *hesed* play in the outcomes of Naomi's story? What part does it play in ours?

9. Contrast the end of our adventure (4:13–17) with the beginning (1:1–5). What are your observations and conclusions?

10. Describe Naomi's relationship with Ruth and Boaz's son from 4:16.

11. Why do you think the townswomen praised God with the words, "Naomi has a son!" (4:17) instead of "Ruth and Boaz have a son!"?

12. Verse 17 tells us that "they" named him Obed. Who do you think had a say in the boy's naming and why?

The theme of sacrificial loyal love, *hesed*, like a scarlet thread, runs through every page of the book of Ruth. Jesus told us that the whole law can be summed up in the Great Commandment, "'Love the Lord your God with all your heart and with all your soul and with all your mind.' . . . [And] 'Love your neighbor as yourself'" (Matthew 22:37–39). We show others our love for God when we lay down our lives in *hesed* for those around us as Jesus laid down his life for us. As you sift through all you've learned on our adventure together, my fervent hope and prayer is that your biggest applicational takeaway is to live out *hesed* every day, knowing that God knows, cares, and knits together a beautiful portrait of every life lived in faith. I've experienced anxiety melting away more and more as my faith grows.   —Sue

Normally, Hebrew genealogies only included the names of men, but Jesus's genealogy includes five women. The inclusion of each of these women reflects the heart of God. Now that you have studied the story of Ruth, make it your goal to learn about the stories of the other women (Tamar, Rahab, Bathsheba [Uriah's wife], and Mary, Jesus's mother). Each of these women faced overwhelming challenges, yet each played a significant role in God's kingdom work. Never forget that God sees and loves you just as much as he does these women, and he has an important role for you to play in his kingdom work as well. —Sue

13. Our adventure ends with the genealogy of the family line beginning with their ancestor Perez and ending with Obed's grandson David. What's amazing about this ending? Why do you think the book ends this way?

14. Turn to the first page of the New Testament, Matthew 1:1–16. Here you find the genealogy of Jesus the Messiah, the son of David. Note the people listed from our adventure in verses 3 through 6 and the final Person listed in verse 16. What do you learn about God's sovereignty from the genealogy of Jesus?

15. Boaz's great-grandson David was one of Israel's greatest kings, and God made him a promise in 2 Samuel 7:16. What was the promise? How was it fulfilled (Luke 1:26–33)?

16. When David learned what God was going to do through his lineage, he burst into prayer and praise in 2 Samuel 7:18–22. How does his prayer reflect what you have learned through your study in the book of Ruth?

17. We've journeyed with Naomi, Ruth, and Boaz through their stories. Consider your story. How is God's providence evident in your life?

18. What have you learned in this study that encourages you to persevere through difficult circumstances and in your quest to know God better and to live a life characterized by less anxiety and more *hesed*?

19. Revisit our adventure in your mind and heart. How have you seen God's attributes below illustrated in the book of Ruth?

God as Merciful

God as Holy

God as Judge

God as Rewarder

God as Sovereign

20. Think back over your study of the book of Ruth. What is your main takeaway? What will you remember next year? Five years from now? Ten years from now? Why is this "big idea" important in your life right now? What do you plan to do about what you learned?

If you are early in your story and waiting to see God's providential work in your life, remember that Naomi and Ruth spent many years watching and waiting to see God's hand at work. Ruth spent those years trusting God and living out *hesed* to those around her. And although Naomi succumbed to discouragement for a time, later she processed her pain, renewed her faith in God's care, and learned to live out *hesed* in her daily life. And Boaz, a picture of true godly masculinity, used his influence to raise up others in beautiful illustrations of Christlike sacrifice. In our quick-fix microwave world, too often we expect instant results, but when it comes to what really matters, "quick" is not God's way. So get on your knees, get outside yourself, live *hesed* at every turn, trust God's providence, and prepare for some beautiful serendipities. —Sue

She left her father and mother, and the land of her nativity,
to come and trust under the shadow of God's wings; and she
had indeed a full reward given her, as Boaz wished; for besides
immediate spiritual blessings to her own soul, and eternal rewards
in another world, she was rewarded with plentiful, and prosperous
outward circumstances, in the family of Boaz; and God raised up
David and Solomon of her seed, and established the crown of Israel
(the people that she chose before her own people) in her posterity,
and (which is much more) of her seed he raised up Jesus Christ, in
whom all families of the earth are blessed.
JONATHAN EDWARDS ("Ruth's Resolution," 308–309)

Optional Extended Study

God Speaks to Your Anxiety: Psalm 91

We don't know who wrote Psalm 91, but the psalm comes alive for me when I envision it as the testimony of a woman experiencing freedom from anxiety. She has learned to process her distressing emotions with the help of her loving heavenly Father. In addition, I like to use feminine pronouns when I read verses 14–16 and in the lesson to make the psalm more personal for women. And I've named the author Free. I hope this approach works for you too.

Free has grown in her faith through an intimate relationship with God and now she rests and trusts in him even during situations that used to lead to nail-biting and white knuckles. Anxiety no longer gets the best of her. Free's voice in Psalm 91 has helped me immeasurably when I feel my emotions rising up in an attempt to distort my good sense. I pray it will minister to you as well.

We observe two speakers in the psalm, Free and Almighty God. First, we will hear from Free and then God will respond.

 Read Psalm 91.

FREE SPEAKS IN PSALM 91:1–13

To oust anxiety, dwell where you belong.

1. Free begins her testimony by telling us that to overcome anxiety we must *dwell* in a specific place (91:1). Where does she live and where does she encourage us to live? What do you think she means?

OPTIONAL

Memorize Jeremiah 29:11–13

"For I know the plans I have for you," declares the Lord, "plans to prosper you and not to harm you, plans to give you hope and a future. Then you will call on me and come and pray to me, and I will listen to you. You will seek me and find me when you seek me with all your heart."

This remarkable psalm speaks with great specificity, and yet with a kind of porousness, so that the language is enormously open to each one's particular experience. Its tone is somewhat instructional, as though reassuring someone else who is unsure. Yet the assurance is not didactic, but confessional. It is a personal testimony of someone whose own experience makes the assurance of faith convincing and authentic.
—Walter Brueggemann (*The Message of the Psalms*, 156)

73

An analogy is a literary device where the author uses symbols, objects, or mental pictures to compare one thing to another. Psalm 91 is full of analogies.   —Sue

What does it mean to dwell?

DIGGING DEEPER

The author uses two different names to describe God in verse 1: "Most High" and "Almighty." What can you learn about the meaning of both names and what do they tell us about the author's relationship with God?

In what sense can God be your "shelter"?

How close must you stand to someone to be in their shadow? What do you learn from this word picture about the interplay between your relationship with God and the struggle to overcome anxiety?

To oust anxiety, be faithful.

2. What does Free do in verses 2 and 9 to delight her heavenly Father?

3. In verse 2, she uses two more word pictures to proclaim how she views God. What are the two word pictures, what do they mean, and what do you think she is communicating by using them?

4. Are you comfortable talking to other believers about your relationship with God? Nonbelievers? What about listening to them? Why or why not? If you have learned how to enter into natural conversations about God with others, please share suggestions with the group.

Our Creator God feels every emotion that healthy human parents experience toward their children. He delights when we call to him like a nursing child cries out for mother's milk. Like a protective parent, Almighty God (El Shaddai) reveals his fierce passion to protect us. His heart stirs on our behalf, especially when we acknowledge him. His ferocious desire to guard us heightens when we acknowledge him and call out to him (91:14–15). Understanding this reality should send us all running to his shelter and living in his shadow. But, like a loving parent, God also grieves and is disappointed when we rebel because he knows the harm we will ultimately bring on ourselves. Tough love, severe mercies, may sometimes be his kindest response. Keep these truths in mind as you continue your study of Psalm 91. —Sue

5. Look ahead to God's responses to Free in verses 14 and 15. What else does a faithful believer do that brings God great joy?

6. Do you love God? If so, why? How do you express that love to him?

7. Do you call on him in good times and bad? Who do you talk to first when you receive a dreaded phone call? Why do you think God wants to communicate with you? What hinders you calling on him?

To oust anxiety, trust in your Father's protective care.

8. In verses 3 and 4, Free describes specific ways God has protected her. What analogies does she use?

What's a fowler's snare?

What's deadly pestilence?

What's a rampart?

9. Imagine you are a helpless baby chick. What kind of protection does a mother bird provide? What does this reveal about God's desire to protect you?

DIGGING DEEPER

The Bible reveals another way God sometimes disciplines disobedient Christians. What can you surmise from the following verses: 1 Corinthians 5:4–5; 11:29–30; Numbers 3:2–4?

10. Under what kinds of circumstances do you think God might choose not to protect his beloved child from trials and struggles? Why?

Proverbs 3:11–12

DIGGING DEEPER

In 1 John 5:16–17, John talks about "sin that leads to death" and "sin that does not lead to death." See also Matthew 12:31, 32 where Jesus mentions a sin that will not be forgiven. Distinguish between sin that leads to death, sin that does not lead to death, and the sin that will not be forgiven.

Hebrews 12:7–11

Philippians 2:14–15

11. In verses 5 through 8, Free uses battle language to express the beauty of God's constant protection. What "time" words do you observe in verses 5 and 6? What does her use of words that speak about time say to you?

12. Why do you think Free specifically talks about fear in "the terror of night"? Have you experienced a similar fear? If so, describe what you felt. Share any ways you have experienced God's comfort and care in the night.

13. What do you think Free is attempting to communicate to you in verses 7 and 8?

I believe this verse [1 John 5:16–17] is teaching that some sins bring God's swift judgment, and result in the premature physical death of the sinner (e.g., Acts 5:1–11; 1 Cor. 5:5; 11:30). Others do not. The fact that it is very difficult, if not impossible, for us *today* to distinguish these types of sins, should not lead us to conclude that a distinction does not exist (cf. Heb. 6:4–6; 10:26–29).
—Tom Constable (*Notes on 1 John*, 115)

The unpardonable sin is not rejection of the Lord Jesus, until the rejecter dies in his unbelief. Such a sin will not be forgiven throughout eternity, but it is not the same sin as that which Jesus condemned with these words: "Anyone who blasphemes against me, the Son of Man, can be forgiven, but blasphemy against the Holy Spirit will never be forgiven, either in this world or in the world to come" (Mt 12:32, NLT). Numerous passages repeat the warning that unbelief in the Savior results in eternal death (Jn 3:18, 36; 1 Jn 5:12; Rv 20:15; 21:8), but these Scriptures do not directly speak of the unpardonable sin. Jesus asserted that a person could be an unbeliever in him, even to the degree of speaking against him, yet not be guilty of the unpardonable sin.
—Philip Comfort and Walter Elwell ("The Unpardonable Sin," *Tyndale Bible Dictionary*)

14. What do you think Free is actually promising in verses 9 and 10? Does verse 10 mean that faithful Christians will never experience trials and troubles? If not, what do you think it means?

No temptation has overtaken you except what is common to mankind. And God is faithful; he will not let you be tempted beyond what you can bear. But when you are tempted, he will also provide a way out so that you can endure it.
—1 Corinthians 10:13

In verse 10, Free writes, "no harm will overtake you, no disaster will come near your tent." To interpret this verse correctly we must dissect the words carefully. She's not saying that when she dwells close to God and tells others about him, nothing bad ever happens to her. We know that's not true simply by looking at the lives of devout men and women in the Bible. Clearly they were not immune to troubles. So what does this passage mean? She says no harm will "overtake" you. If you overtake me in a race, you gain on me and win the race. Let's say you are a kidnapper and I'm running for my life. If you overpower me, then I'm at your mercy. The author reveals that anxiety need not overpower or overtake us when we remain close to God.

A disaster is an overwhelming event that ends in destruction and devastation, like a forest fire or tsunami. God wants us to know that when we abide in him, ultimately nothing can destroy or overpower us. Grasping this truth can greatly lessen our anxiety when we face trials and struggles. She doesn't say that what happens won't hurt. But God promises to be with us in it, soothing our tears and giving us a sense of peace and rest. However, we must not forget the qualifiers: dwelling close enough to God to be "in his shadow," loving and calling out to him in distress, and not remaining silent about our faith.

To oust anxiety, trust in angelic care.

15. Free has seen God's supernatural hand at work through his angels in verses 11–13. What does she reveal about the ministry of God's angels in the world?

16. We are often unable to observe the work of God's angels in our lives. Nevertheless, have you ever experienced what you believe was the presence or protection of angels? Do you know someone who has? What happened and how were you or others affected?

Angels protect from physical harm and give believers strength to overcome difficulties, pictured here as wild lions and dangerous snakes.
—A. P. Ross ("Psalms," *The Bible Knowledge Commentary*, 860)

The writer was using hyperbole when he wrote that the believer will not even stub his or her toe (v. 12; see also Mark 16:18; Luke 10:19; Acts 28:1–6). Verse 13 also seems to be hyperbolic. It pictures overcoming dangerous animals. God has given some believers this kind of protection occasionally (e.g., Daniel 6; Acts 28:3–6), but the writer's point was that God will protect his people from all kinds of dangers.

Satan quoted verses 11 and 12 when he tempted Jesus in the wilderness (Matthew 4:6). He urged Jesus to interpret this promise literally. However, Jesus declined to tempt God by deliberately putting himself in a dangerous situation to see if God would miraculously deliver him.

Jesus referred to verse 13 when He sent the disciples out on a preaching mission (Luke 10:19). Again, it seems clear that His intention was to assure the disciples that God would take care of them. He was not encouraging them to put their lives in danger deliberately.
—Tom Constable (*Notes on Psalms*, 330)

DIGGING DEEPER

What can you learn about angels from the following passages: Genesis 3:24, 28:10–12; Psalm 148:1–5; Matthew 25:31; Mark 1:12–13; 1 Timothy 3:16, 5:21; Hebrews 1:3–4; 1 Peter 1:12; Revelation 1:17–20, 14:6–20, 15:5–8?

Angels are real, and they aren't pretty little cherubs with wings who sit around on clouds all day strumming harps. They are powerful wingless majestic beings who carry out God's desires. My drive into the campus where I teach is often a 45-minute journey on a busy highway. Often I pray for God's angels to surround my vehicle as I come and go, and I sense their presence protecting me. We have no idea how many times during our lives that angels lift us up out of harm's way or orchestrate situations for our good. It's incredibly comforting to realize that we are indestructible until our loving heavenly Father determines otherwise. Do you believe that? I have found that truth to be a beautiful antidote to anxiety. —Sue

NOW GOD SPEAKS

To oust anxiety, believe your Father's words.

17. In verses 14 and 15, God reveals several ways he protected Free as she dwelt in his shelter and shadow. What do you think these promises might look like in your life?

I will rescue her

I will protect her

I will answer her

I will be with her

I will deliver her

The writer recorded God's promise to deliver those who know and love Him. He will eventually answer the cries for help that His people voice (cf. 50:15; Joel 2:32; Acts 2:21; Rom. 10:13). He will not abandon them in their distresses (cf. Josh. 1:9; Matt. 28:20). The promises of rescue and honor normally find fulfillment in this life, but they always do the other side of the grave.
—Tom Constable (*Notes on Psalms*, 330)

I will honor her

18. God promised Free that he would satisfy her with long life (91:16). In light of the reality that some faithful Christians die young, what do you think he meant?

The [person] described in this psalm fills out the measure of [her] days, and whether [she] dies young or old [she] is quite satisfied with life, and content to leave it.
—Charles Spurgeon (*Psalms Volume II*, 30)

19. Finally, God promises Free that he will show her his salvation. Salvation in the Bible has a number of different meanings, so we need to figure out what we think the author meant by the context. See several examples of different meanings in the sidebar. Which meaning(s) do you think best fits the context?

Salvation in the Bible can mean 1) saved from the penalty of sin by believing in Christ's work on the cross for eternal life 2) saved in battle 3) saved from physical sickness or physical death in this life 4) saved from the consequences of sin in this life 5) saved out of trials and troubles. —Sue

The full sight of divine grace shall be [her] closing vision. Not with destruction before [her] black as night, but with salvation bright as noonday smiling upon [her], [she] shall enter into [her] rest.
—Charles Spurgeon
(*Psalms Volume II*, 30)

20. How do you feel as you conclude your study of Psalm 91? Encouraged? Discouraged? Challenged? Another emotion not listed here? Why do you think you are experiencing these emotions? What do you think your loving heavenly Father wants you to do with these emotions?

Therefore, there is now no condemnation for those who are in Christ Jesus, because through Christ Jesus the law of the Spirit who gives life has set you free from the law of sin and death.
—Romans 8:1–2

21. How might this psalm help you overcome crippling anxiety in your life? How might you help others overcome it?

If we claim to be without sin, we deceive ourselves and the truth is not in us. If we confess our sins, he is faithful and just and will forgive us our sins and purify us from all unrighteousness.
—1 John 1:8–9

You may have periods of darkness or of doubt.
You may encounter painful struggle and discouragement.
But there will also be moments of exultation and glory.
And most important of all,
you will become free.
JOHN WHITE (*The Fight*, 1)

Jesus Speaks to Your Anxiety

For many women, anxiety is just part of the process of resolving problems and anticipating or preparing for future events. The flow of anxious thoughts is relentless. They distract. They intrude. They generate a series of catastrophic hypothetical scenarios and we get caught up in the what-if implications. We conjure up the emotions that might accompany the event until we make ourselves sick. Muscles tense. Stomachs tighten with a heavy sinking ache. Necks seize up. The enemy throws a party and we are shackled to our imaginations. We've wasted the opportunity to use our time productively. We've exhausted ourselves emotionally, leaving little time to worship God, enjoy, create, and serve.

The word *anxious* means to be torn apart—to be held in suspense. It comes from a picture of a ship tossed convulsing in a raging storm. The English word comes from an old Anglo Saxon term meaning to strangle. If someone is strangling you, you can't think about much else. Anxiety drains us of energy. It saps our strength. There's nothing noble about it and everything foolish, yet it's easy to do. I've been there.

When I became a Christian at age twenty-four, I carried a bad habit into my new life in Christ. I was anxious about everything. I thought worry and anxiety showed how much I cared. What helped me break this debilitating habit? A mentor helped me understand that anxiety was evidence that I did not trust God, and it was sin.

Her challenge caused me to rethink my assumptions, and I began to change. In addition, my immersion in God's Word over the years loosed the stranglehold of anxiety in my life and ultimately opened the floodgates of peace. Also, I identified my gift-mix, the spiritual gifts God has given me, and the way God wired me, which led to a fervent desire to serve him. I stepped outside my fear and began to do something for the kingdom, bringing a sense of purpose to my life. All these elements combined to help me leave the habit of anxiety behind. It creeps back in sometimes when difficulties invade my life, but I've learned to battle them early before they can grip my emotions and get the best of me.

In this lesson on discovering victory over anxiety, Jesus helps us

OPTIONAL

Memorize Philippians 4:4–7

Rejoice in the Lord always. I will say it again: Rejoice! Let your gentleness be evident to all. The Lord is near. Do not be anxious about anything, but in every situation, by prayer and petition, with thanksgiving, present your requests to God. And the peace of God, which transcends all understanding, will guard your hearts and your minds in Christ Jesus.

unravel the mystery of an anxiety-free, peace-packed life—a precious gift found only in God.

 **Read Luke 12:22–34.**

1. Jesus began his teaching on breaking the habit of worry and anxiety by refocusing our lives on what's really important. What does he say not to worry about (12:22–23)?

Jesus begins with a call not to worry. The Greek present imperative used here implies that we should be constantly free of anxiety. We are subject to God's care, so we should rest in his hands. . . . We should not be excessively distracted about our physical circumstances, for food and clothes are but the wrapping paper around which true life revolves.
—Darrell Bock (*NIV Application Commentary: Luke*, 349)

2. Do you agree with Jesus that these needs are not worth our worry? Why or why not? In what sense are they important? In what sense are they not nearly as important as other issues?

3. Is Jesus encouraging us to be lazy and not work to provide for our needs? What do the following passages reveal about the place and value of work in our lives?

Genesis 2:15

Ecclesiastes 5:18–20

2 Thessalonians 3:6–13

4. Since the Bible instructs us to work to supply our needs, what is Jesus's main point in Luke 12:22–23?

5. How much of your life is spent feeling anxious about physical needs?

Jesus and his disciples are probably outside enjoying nature. Now Jesus uses several object lessons to illustrate his teaching.

6. Imagine Jesus pointing to a big black crow-like raven, considered unclean and useless. What does Jesus say about them in verse 24?

7. If ravens were an unclean and useless bird, how much more valuable are you to your heavenly Father? Deep down in your heart, how precious do you really believe you are to God (Romans 8:32)? Why or why not? How does your answer to this question influence your ability to overcome habitual anxiety?

8. Jesus asks you two questions in Luke 12:25–26. What are your answers to these questions? How much does anxiety actually accomplish?

Hyperbole is a literary device used by authors to accentuate a point. Sometimes Jesus used hyperbole in his teaching— overstatement for the sake of effect. For example in the Sermon on the Mount, when Jesus taught on the dangers of lust, he said, "If your right eye causes you to stumble, gouge it out and throw it away . . . and if your right hand causes you to stumble, cut it off and throw it away . . . (Matthew 5:29–30). He was not suggesting bodily mutilation but to take these dangers seriously.   —Sue

9. If anxiety is profitless and useless, why do you think so many women today allow themselves to be enslaved by it? Are you one of them?

10. How do you think anxiety effects our physical bodies? Is it possible that habitual anxiety might shorten your lifespan?

DIGGING DEEPER

Read *The Body Keeps the Score* by Bessel A. van der Kolk (Penguin Books) to learn more about the impact of anxiety on our physical health.

11. Jesus turns and points to another object lesson from nature (12:27). What is it and what can you learn from this example of God's creation?

12. Jesus compared this object lesson to "Solomon in all his splendor." Describe Solomon's attempt to out-beautify nature from 2 Chronicles 9:15–21. Do you think he succeeded? Why or why not? What's the lesson for us?

The flowers (*Gr. krinon*) cannot do anything whatsoever to provide for their own needs. They are totally dependent on God. Still He provides for them and does so magnificently. He gives every common flower more glorious clothing than "Solomon," Israel's most glorious king, could provide for himself. Toiling and spinning to provide clothing seems to be in view. This was women's work in Jesus' day, in contrast to providing for the young (v. 24), which was men's work. Thus Jesus implied that His teaching was applicable to both male and female disciples.
—Tom Constable
(*Notes on Luke*, 286)

13. What is the difference between wildflowers and the grass of the field? What do you think Jesus might be communicating by using these two different examples?

14. Jesus issues a strong rebuke to any of his followers who allow themselves to live with habitual anxiety in Luke 12:28. What does he say and how do you feel about his rather stern admonition? Why do you think he feels so strongly about our overcoming anxiety in our lives?

A little bit of reflection helps us to recognize that most worry is about things that can't be changed (the past), things that can't be controlled (the present), or things that might not happen (the future).
—Walter Liefeld ("Luke," 963)

15. Who sets a bad example for us? What illustrations come to mind? Why are we not to emulate them? (12:30)

Worry happens when we assume responsibility God never intended us to have. You may be thinking, *If we don't worry, how will I feed and clothe my family? Isn't worry a good motivator? Doesn't it help to keep us on track?* The answer to these questions is a resounding NO!
—Vickie Kraft (*Facing Your Feelings*, 74)

16. What is God's ultimate antidote to anxiety (12:31)? What does this involve?

17. What negative emotion often accompanies embracing this antidote to anxiety (12:32)? Why? Is this emotion hindering you from experiencing victory over anxiety?

18. Again Jesus uses a bit of hyperbole to grab our attention in verse 33 when he says, "Sell your possessions and give to the poor." What's his point? Why is this wise counsel?

19. Jesus ends this teaching with a gripping statement—"For where your treasure is, there your heart will be also" (12:34). What is your treasure? How does this reality impact your spiritual and emotional health, particularly anxiety?

20. How would your life change if you took Jesus's counsel to heart by seeking God's kingdom on earth and in heaven as your priority and focus?

21. Think back on your study of Ruth, Psalm 91, and Jesus's counsel on anxiety in Luke 12:22–34. What have you learned that you will carry forward to help you discover victory over habitual anxiety?

We can attempt to create a safe environment for our lives.
We can try to create a world where we control others.
We can seek the accolades of peers to give ourselves worth.
We can withdraw so we are safe in our own little world.
We can seek to be different, so we are noticed and affirmed as
present, whether positively or negatively—
a route the teenager makes into a vocation!
Each of these attempts is really an evasion of the need
to seek identity in the one source who can give it,
. . . God.
DARRELL L. BOCK (*The NIV Application Commentary: Luke*, 352)

Works Cited

Bisagno, John. *God Is*. Wheaton, IL: Victor Books, 1983.

Bock, Darrell L. *The NIV Application Commentary: Luke*. Grand Rapids: Zondervan, 1996.

Brueggemann, Walter. *The Message of the Psalms*. Minneapolis, MN: Augsburg Press, 1984.

Campbell Jr., Edward F. *Ruth: A New Translation with Introduction and Commentary*. Vol. 7 of *The Anchor Bible*, edited by William Foxwell Albright and David Noel Freedman. New York: Doubleday, 1975.

Chambers, Rick, and Tracy Bloom. "OC Paramedic Helps Rescue Doctor Who Saved His Life as Baby; Pair Reunited." *KTLA 5 News*, March 29, 2015. https://ktla.com/2015/03/29/oc-paramedic-helps-rescue-doctor-who-saved-his-life-as-baby-pair-reunited/

Chisholm Jr., Robert B. *A Commentary on Judges and Ruth*. Grand Rapids: Kregel Academic, 2013.

Comfort, Philip W., and Walter A. Elwell. "Unpardonable Sin." In *Tyndale Bible Dictionary*. Wheaton, IL: Tyndale, 2001.

Constable, Tom. *Notes on 1 John*. Plano Bible Chapel. 2020 edition. https://planobiblechapel.org/tcon/notes/pdf/1john.pdf.

———. *Notes on Luke*. Plano Bible Chapel. 2020 edition. https://planobiblechapel.org/tcon/notes/pdf/luke.pdf.

———. *Notes on Psalms*. Plano Bible Chapel. 2020 edition. https://planobiblechapel.org/tcon/notes/pdf/psalms.pdf.

Custis James, Carolyn. *The Gospel of Ruth: Loving God Enough to Break the Rules*. Grand Rapids: Zondervan, 2008.

Dickason, C. Fred. *Angels Elect and Evil*. Chicago: Moody Press, 1975.

Edwards, Jonathan. "Ruth's Resolution." In *Sermons and Discourses, 1734–1738*, edited by M. X. Lesser. Vol. 19 of *Works of Jonathan Edwards Online*. http://edwards.yale.edu/archive?path=aHR0cDovL2Vkd2FyZHMueWFsZS5lZHUvY2dpLWJpbi9uZXdwaGlsby9nZXRvYmplY3QucGw/Yy4xODoxMy53amVv.

Hendricks, Howard G., and William D. Hendricks. *Living by the Book*. Chicago: Moody Press, 2007.

Jeffers, Susan. *Feel the Fear and Do It Anyway.* New York: Ballantine, 1987.

Jensen, Irving L. *Judges and Ruth: A Self-Study Guide.* Chicago: Moody Press, 1987.

Kraft, Vickie. *Facing Your Feelings: Moving from Emotional Bondage to Spiritual Freedom.* Dallas: Word, 1996.

Legaspi, Marnie. "Ruth: The So-Called Scandal." In *Vindicating the Vixens: Revisiting Sexualized, Vilified, and Marginalized Women of the Bible,* edited by Sandra Glahn, 59–80. Grand Rapids: Kregel Academic, 2017.

Liefeld, Walter L. "Luke." In *Matthew, Mark, Luke.* Vol. 8 of *The Expositor's Bible Commentary,* edited by Frank E. Gaebelein and J. D. Douglas. Grand Rapids: Zondervan, 1984.

Manley, G. T. *The New Bible Handbook.* Chicago: InterVarsity, 1949.

Mathews, Alice. *A Woman God Can Lead.* Grand Rapids: Discovery House, 1998.

Minirth, Frank, Paul Meier, and Don Hawkins. *Worry-Free Living.* Nashville: Thomas Nelson, 1989.

Moore, Michael S. "To King or Not to King: A Canonical-Historical Approach to Ruth." *Bulletin for Biblical Research* 11, no. 1 (2001): 27–41.

Morgan, G. Campbell. *The Gospel According to Luke.* Old Tappen, NJ: Fleming H. Revell Company, 1931.

Newman, Tim. "Anxiety in the West: Is It on the Rise?" Medical News Today. September 5, 2018. www.medicalnewstoday.com/articles/322877.php.

Roche, Arthur Somers. *The Harper Book of Quotations.* 3rd ed. Edited by Robert I. Fitzhenry. New York: HarperCollins, 1993.

Ross, A. P. "Psalms." In *The Bible Knowledge Commentary: An Exposition of the Scriptures* (Vol. 1), edited by J. F. Walvoord and R. B. Zuck. Wheaton, IL: Victor, 1985.

Sangster, Margaret E. "The Christmas Tree." *Elocutionist's Journal* 11 (January 1878): 1.

Spurgeon, Charles. *Psalms Volume II.* Crossway Classic Commentaries, edited by Alister McGrath and J. I. Packer. Wheaton, IL: Crossway, 1993.

Swindoll, Charles R. *The Swindoll Study Bible.* Carol Stream, IL: Tyndale, 2017.

Tucker, Ruth A. *Dynamic Women of the Bible: What We Can Learn from Their Surprising Stories.* Grand Rapids: Baker, 2014.

White, John. *The Fight.* Downers Grove, IL: InterVarsity, 1976.

About the Author

S ue Edwards is professor of educational ministries and leadership (her specialization is women's studies) at Dallas Theological Seminary, where she has the opportunity to equip men and women for future ministry. She brings more than forty years of experience into the classroom as a Bible teacher, curriculum writer, and overseer of several megachurch women's ministries. As minister to women at Irving Bible Church and director of women's ministry at Prestonwood Baptist Church in Dallas, she has worked with women from all walks of life, ages, and stages. Her passion is to see modern and postmodern women connect, learn from one another, and bond around God's Word. Her Bible studies have ushered thousands of women all over the country and overseas into deeper Scripture study and community experiences.

With Kelley Mathews, Sue has coauthored *Organic Ministry to Women: A Guide to Transformational Ministry with Next Generation Women*, *Women's Retreats: A Creative Planning Guide* (with coauthor Linda Robinson), and *Leading Women Who Wound: Strategies for an Effective Ministry*. Sue and Kelley joined with Henry Rogers to coauthor *Mixed Ministry: Working Together as Brothers and Sisters in an Oversexed Society*. *Organic Mentoring: A Mentor's Guide to Relationships with Next Generation Women*, coauthored with Barbara Neumann, explores the new values, preferences, and problems of the next generation and shows mentors how to avoid potential land mines and how to mentor successfully. Her newest book, coedited with DTS vice president, dean of students, and professor of educational ministries and leadership George M. Hillman Jr., *Invitation to Educational Ministry: Foundations of Transformative Christian Education*, serves as a primary academic textbook for schools all over the country as well as a handbook for church leaders.

Sue has a doctor of ministry degree from Gordon–Conwell Theological Seminary in Boston, a master's in Bible from Dallas Theological Seminary, and a bachelor's degree in journalism from Trinity University. With Dr. Joye Baker, she oversees the Dallas Theological Seminary doctor of ministry degree in educational ministry with a women-in-ministry emphasis.

Sue has been married to David for forty-seven years. They have two married daughters, Heather and Rachel, and five grandchildren. David is a retired CAD applications engineer and a lay prison chaplain. Sue loves fine chocolates and exotic coffees, romping with her grandchildren, and taking walks with David and her two West Highland terriers, Quigley and Emma Jane.

Notes

Notes

Notes

Notes

Notes

Notes

Notes

Notes

Notes

Notes

Notes

Notes

The Discover Together Bible Study Series

Inductive Bible studies for women from Sue Edwards

Daniel: Discovering the Courage to Stand for Your Faith
Philippians: Discovering Joy Through Relationship
Ecclesiastes: Discovering Meaning in a Meaningless World
Galatians: Discovering Freedom in Christ Through Daily Practice

And many more!

Learn more at DiscoverTogetherSeries.com

KREGEL PUBLICATIONS

Trusted, biblically based resources

TAKE YOUR FIRST STEPS ON YOUR PATH OF EXTRAORDINARY PURPOSE

Every day, we're called to choose whether we will take the path God calls us to or follow our own way. Through this ten-week Bible study, Jodie Niznik invites you to take an experiential journey along with Moses to learn just what that choice can mean—and how it can change your life.

The new Real People, Real Faith Bible Study series combines inductive study with practical spiritual disciplines. Take a fresh look at old stories that have a real connection to your life today!

Trusted, biblically based resources